# *Daily Ripples*

## JOHN L. WAGNER

**BALBOA.**PRESS
A DIVISION OF HAY HOUSE

Copyright © 2021 John L. Wagner.

All rights reserved. No part of this book may be used or reproduced by any means, graphic, electronic, or mechanical, including photocopying, recording, taping or by any information storage retrieval system without the written permission of the author except in the case of brief quotations embodied in critical articles and reviews.

Balboa Press books may be ordered through booksellers or by contacting:

Balboa Press
A Division of Hay House
1663 Liberty Drive
Bloomington, IN 47403
www.balboapress.com
844-682-1282

Because of the dynamic nature of the Internet, any web addresses or links contained in this book may have changed since publication and may no longer be valid. The views expressed in this work are solely those of the author and do not necessarily reflect the views of the publisher, and the publisher hereby disclaims any responsibility for them.

The author of this book does not dispense medical advice or prescribe the use of any technique as a form of treatment for physical, emotional, or medical problems without the advice of a physician, either directly or indirectly. The intent of the author is only to offer information of a general nature to help you in your quest for emotional and spiritual well-being. In the event you use any of the information in this book for yourself, which is your constitutional right, the author and the publisher assume no responsibility for your actions.

Any people depicted in stock imagery provided by Getty Images are models, and such images are being used for illustrative purposes only.
Certain stock imagery © Getty Images.

Print information available on the last page.

ISBN: 978-1-9822-7040-7 (sc)
ISBN: 978-1-9822-7070-4 (hc)
ISBN: 978-1-9822-7071-1 (e)

Library of Congress Control Number: 2021912734

Balboa Press rev. date: 07/15/2021

# Contents

Acknowledgement .................................................................. vii

January ................................................................................... 1
February.............................................................................. 19
March ................................................................................. 37
April.................................................................................... 55
May...................................................................................... 73
June..................................................................................... 91
July ................................................................................... 109
August .............................................................................. 127
September ........................................................................ 145
October............................................................................. 163
November ........................................................................ 181
December ......................................................................... 199

Afterword......................................................................... 217

# Acknowledgement

I am grateful for the loving Spirit that works through the gifts of people, making it possible for us to work together in this loving union. I would like to thank Pam Ribby and Michaela MacGown for their assistance with taking my vision of **Daily Ripples** and turning it into reality. Without your enthusiasm, time, and professional expertise, this book wouldn't be possible. A special thanks goes out to Mary Anne Barnheiser for her help with creating my first book, **Poems and Inspirational Thoughts: Awareness and Encouragement**.

I would like to thank Jody Kunze, Linda Blackmon, and Greg King for their continued support and friendship. I appreciate everyone who has encouraged and inspired me to keep writing, and contributed to my personal growth and life experiences.

Mostly I would like to thank a loving God for pulling me out of my deep despair. Where I thought all hope was lost, You brought me to a new way of living. May I never forget where I came from and the pit that I was brought out of.

# Reflections

# January

# January

### 20/20 Vision

20/20 vision and walking around blind,
Thinking of everything I've loved, lost, and left behind,
Spanned the years, tears, and fears,
Thinking I had 20/20 vision when really, I was blind.
The dark cold day would finally come;
Through a gift of desperation,
I would begin to see,
There was always something watching over me,
And if I had a willingness to start,
There was a book to help me see my part,
And as I read, it plants a seed,
That if I continue, it will lead,
To a new way of life,
So I can see with this new 20/20 vision ahead of me,
How things should really be,
So I can leave that old life behind,
And no longer have to stumble around blind.

## January 1

As old things pass away
and new is continually on the horizon
You prepare us for this day.

## January 2

May this loving Spirit become the desire of my heart,
for this is how we were created.

## January 3

You are revealing your creativity to us in exciting new ways.
We see your hand on everything we touch and we find joy in your presence wherever we go.
Thank you, Jesus.

## January 4

When we live in the light of your loving presence, that light shines through us into the lives of others.

## January 5

Help me to stop focusing on the brokenness in my life, and help fan the flames of Your Love.

## January 6

It is easier to accept the limitation of others when I acknowledge my own. My distorted perception and inconsistent behavior are but just a few.

## January 7

Self-pity and anger can deny me the simplest of pleasures and light-heartedness.
Help me to lighten up and laugh at myself.

## January 8

You are constantly changing and revising us to accomplish new things.
May we ask you to open the eyes of our hearts and minds to the opportunities that you lay out before us.

## January 9

Help my mind become kind and pure
for what I think, I become.

## January 10

Are things I do obscured by clouds of doubt,
rationalization, or self-seeking motives?
Help me seek a true loving path.

## January 11

Teach us to observe all things
To do what's right
for You are with us always.

## January 12

Help me change my selfish common sense
to unselfish common sense.

## January 13

Making positive strides begins with small steps in the right direction.

## January 14

Truly this is a better way to be guided: to come to know more, to be able to trust Love's ways and plans for the development of character in us.

## January 15

May our trust and faith in You grow and provide a
pathway for You to love others through us.

## January 16

We rejoice in Love's gentleness
for Your loving grace is at hand.

## January 17

Instead of questioning what I am getting from life,
may I ask what can I give,
and by doing so, I may find that my self-pity
will be replaced by self-esteem.

## January 18

As You love others through us,
May we learn to love others
as You do.

## January 19

Help me change my complaining to appreciation and gratitude.

## January 20

Help me to nurture healthy thoughts about myself and others, for what I think about I become and see in others.

## January 21

Help me not to speak bad of anyone, avoid quarrelling, be gentle and show courtesy towards all.

## January 22

Patience:
to accept and tolerate delay or troubling situations
without getting angry or upset.
Something I am far from mastering,
and have a long way to go.

## January 23

I turned to drinking and whatever else I could find to overcome my fears, in return it gave me loneliness, pain, and despair.

A loving Creator transforms me over time, and slowly my fears are being replaced with happiness, freedom, and peace, as I live by a new set of principles: Spiritual in nature.

## January 24

You have created beautiful spirits in people, for a beautiful purpose. Help us see these positive qualities in others, our circumstances, as well as ourselves, with an open and loving heart and mind.

## January 25

You teach and help me understand what to value, love, and appreciate in others, as well as myself. Thank you.

## January 26

When Your loving presence becomes the focal point of my consciousness, everything falls into place. I gain a new perspective on life and it becomes meaningful.

## January 27

Love has no limits or conditions for us. It only asks that we seek it, attain it, and receive it's quiet, gentle spirit.

## January 28

Love leads each of us, on a unique and tailor-made path, perfectly suited for our journey through life. Help us choose to stay on Your chosen path.

## January 29

Love does not search out my faults and failures - I do, when I angrily judge myself and others.
May we immerse ourselves in and be receptive to Your loving grace and presence.

## January 30

Help me to become more aware of my rebellious tendencies', resentments, and petty-unpleasant feelings. Bring them into the light of your presence to be free of them – exposed and expelled.

## January 31

If we don't love ourselves in a healthy way,
we will never love others as we should.

# February

# *February*

### A Moonlight Beach

Life can be as gentle as a walk along
A Moonlight Beach, or as stormy as A
Raging Sea, that tosses me to and fro
Emotionally and mentally, and
When this happens, I must find that
Still, small, loving voice from within
That helps me handle any situation I
May find myself in, so I can be at
Peace with both you and me no
Matter what life happens to be.

## February 1

May we Guard well these petitions of Love to our hearts, for they are Great Gifts and may we nurture its Loving presence.

## February 2

May a loving relationship be vibrant and challenging as it reaches into more areas of our lives, that help us grow.

## February 3

**Love**

May Your beliefs, become our Beliefs,
May Your thoughts become our thoughts,
May Your actions become our actions,
Help us to see one another
Through Your Loving eyes.
For I cannot do it on my own.

## February 4

Love, help me accept myself and the choices I have made and not fantasize how I might have done things differently.

## February 5

Help us to be a sanctuary for your loving presence.
May you increase our faith, hope, love, courage
and most of all our passion and love for you
and one another.
May we be uplifting and encouraging to
each other throughout our day,
and may we love our neighbors as ourselves.

## February 6

God, teach me to care about people as you
have cared for me

## February 7

How comforting it is to see Love working through people!

## February 8

When we open up the Book of Love,
the light of Love lets us in.

## February 9

Love desires to help us be of
one mind and one accord,
counting the cost to save the one who is lost,
That when one is lost,
together the ninety-nine will seek to find the one.

## February 10

In your loving presence, we find peace.
You put gladness in our hearts
and a place to lay down in peace.
When we seek you with all our heart,
you are there.

## February 11

Not to be discouraged when many prayers seem
to go yet unanswered,
time is a trainer and teacher of patience and trust.
Sometimes when our circumstances are most
extreme, we are better able to see
The Power of Love
working in our life
when we seek it, we see it

## February 12

When my will is in line with love, there is peace within.

## February 13

I hope the feeling of separation
will one day vanish.
In the meantime, I pray
that faith will keep
us on a loving path.

## February 14

Your love - may we treasure it,
for it is a true compass for us that gets us through
our struggles
and simplifies our lives
and changes the way we see our circumstances.

## February 15

You wean us from
our dependencies,
so that we may find
security in your
loving presence.

## February 16

We look for the things
which are unseen
for the things which are
unseen are eternal.

## February 17

Help me remember -
all things can work together for a pattern of good,
with Love as my guide.

## February 18

Your loving knowledge and understanding,
renews our mind, cleanses our heart and invigorates us.
Thank you for this loving transformation.

# February 19

Anxiousness and difficulties
can be embraced in a calm perspective,
these challenges can be opportunities for growth,
help me to see them in this
New light.

# February 20

May I always be grateful
for this world of light,
love and truth I see
when I allow it to
direct my vision.

## February 21

May we live in union with this peace
That transcends understanding and
be joined in this loving relationship.
Hungering for resolution of all difficulties
is a false hope,
Finding peace in the midst of our difficulties
is a real gift.

## February 22

Love asks –
be merciful, gracious,
slow to anger and abounding in grace.

## February 23

A thankful attitude opens the windows of Heaven,
from which spiritual blessings flow freely.
Thankfulness: the language of love and intimacy.

## February 24

Love-
you teach us to be the rock and not the roll
as you watch and guard over our soul
and rest peacefully upon us.

## February 25

Your way is perfectly and personally designed for us.
Your loving words are a proven shield
to all who trust in You.

## February 26

Bitterness, anger, and unforgiveness will only cause me pain and rob me of peace and end in loneliness. Forgiveness, amends, helping others, and thankfulness can be my way out.

## February 27

May the spirit of truth dwell within us and may we treasure this truth with an everlasting love.

## February 28

Under Your wing and a prayer
we are loved and sheltered there.

# February 29 (Leap Year)

May I look for where God's love is and not where it isn't.

*Reflections*

# March

# March

**Seeds of Love**

May the seeds of love land on fertile hearts,
And not be choked out by the hardness of hate
Or the weeds of contempt and doubt,
But may Love be the voice that is carried out,
That this love will spring forth and grow,
And create fields of loving hearts
That flourish wherever they go,
So that this Love will forever expand and flow,
That Love's wisdom will be the light that we all show.

## March 1

You are a saturated
cloud showering
peace on to the
pools of our mind,
You seek to bless
us and you are the goal
of all our searching.

## March 2

We never know where our shadow will cast.
So may we create
Loving memories that last.

## March 3

Help us to be the kind, understanding, wise, and responsible humanity that You created us to be.

## March 4

When I place myself in your loving hands,
I find emotional stability
If I am reliant on a loving spirit,
I could not play God to myself
Or to my fellows
nor feel the urge to
This new attitude can bring inner strength and
peace that protects me from being shaken by
the shortcomings of myself or others
and calamities, not of my own making.

# March 5

You weave
blessings into our
mundane days and
You prepare us for
any difficulties
that come our way,
as we keep our
focus on You

# March 6

May we come and join with this loving spirit
and learn from it.
For it is gentle and its burden
is light,
and
we will find rest.

## March 7

May we tap into this inner resource of love and guidance, and fasten ourselves to its foundation.

## March 8

Love plants the seeds, carries the message:
LOVE:
L - **Let**
O - **O**thers
V - **Vo**luntarily
E - **E**volve

## March 9

May we rejoice
in being fully
understood in Your
loving presence.

## March 10

May we view each day as an adventure
planned out by a loving guide
knowing that a thankful heart
helps and changes
our perspective.

# March 11

May we be as one,
for You are our route and the vine
and we are the branches
for together we bear much fruit and
become whole.

May we take the time to refresh
ourselves in Your loving presence,
and feel the peace You offer us.

# March 12

You help us over-come
the Goliath's in our lives
though we may not have the experience,
our faith, trust, and Your gentle guidance
will give us success

# March 13

May we allow You to permeate our thoughts
with your radiant presence,
allowing us to become channels
of your Love, Hope, Faith, Courage, and Truth

# March 14

Your Radiance and shimmering presence
calls softly to our consciousness,
gently seeking entrance to our innermost being,
for You are infinitely tender and gentle
Your Light reaches into our dark, and
You give us hope

# March 15

Love is our refuge, it's Grace shows in
countless places and situations,
it showers blessings and outright miracles
on our planet.
As we grow closer to its loving presence,
It opens our eyes to these wonderful
Sights, sounds, and the shifting shades of light.

# March 16

Love –
You reveal virtues and actions
I wish I had and
hope to someday attain.

## March 17

When I put my trust in your loving presence
even my mistakes and sins
can be recycled into something good
through your transforming grace
and with a thankful attitude
in your presence nothing is wasted.

## March 18

May we breathe in your presence, breathe in your air,
and breathe in your love, for you truly care.

## March 19

May we be a prince or princess of vagabonds
and carry His loving message on and on and on
building a stairway to heaven for others
before we are gone.

## March 20

You have been my help in the shadow of your wings.
I will rejoice.

## March 21

You are keenly aware of my helplessness.
You go before me and alongside me
and I am not alone.
Worries and fears are transformed into
Faith and Serenity.

## March 22

May we clear the static from our minds and hear
Your loving voice above all else and the plans
You have for us.

# March 23

May the light of your presence
shine on any pursuit you have set before us
and let it not become idle or get between us
help us to see things from your perspective

# March 24

May I seek you for evermore!
May I always remember
the marvelous works and wonders
You have done in my life
and the lives of others around the world

## March 25

Let me not be possessive
of people and things
but let me seek to possess
Your perception
of the world and the people in it

## March 26

Though we are in earthly vessels,
you designed us to be filled with heavenly contents –
love, joy and peace
we find in Your loving presence.

## March 27

Our we tongue tied and twisted,
letting loving words, just go whistling by?

## March 28

Love's radiant fruits
of joy, peace, kindness, goodwill,
faithfulness, gentleness, and self-control,
wants to bring these virtues into our innermost-
being and into the depths of our soul.

## March 29

You give us a new set of glasses
in which to see the world and our circumstances
You also give us a new set of ears
in which to hear your gentle voice
in the sounds of music

## March 30

Love you are a wonderful and beautiful symphony
that knows how to orchestrate us
through the highs and lows of our lives
till we become the loving masterpiece
You created us to be

# March 31

When I stopped blaming everything and everyone
for the way my life had turned out
and took responsibility for my choices in life,
that's when healing and growth began

# April

# April

### Spring of Life

May we draw from the spring of life,
That we, too, may spring forth and flow,
On to others that may also grow,
So that all our springs may one day find,
That we were all meant to be combined.

# April 1

You prepare us for the day that stretches out
before us,
as we spend quality time with You,
in Your presence,
Through communication,
You equip us for the
journey ahead, for
You are our loving
companion.

# April 2

You are the shepherd of our souls,
In you, may we always console.

## April 3

May our words and actions
lead us to You
and may Your words change us from the inside out

## April 4

If I don't want people looking at my faults,
I shouldn't be looking at theirs.

## April 5

Take my -Not Enoughs-
and my -What Ifs-
and make them something more,
something to live for

## April 6

Love does the miraculous and chooses to involve us.
May we place our broken lives, frailties, failure,
our pain and suffering in your loving hands
and be surprised with the fullness you reveal.

## April 7

Love gives courage, understanding and wisdom to deal with fear, pain, and risk of life.

## April 8

Life - what adventure Love has planned. May we be in tuned to this loving journey.

## April 9

Your guiding light illuminates our path
as you walk alongside us,
strengthening and encouraging us
as we gain loving confidence in our daily walk
with You.

## April 10

If I am to be chained,
let these links connect me to
hope, trusting, waiting, knowing and seeing
of Loves return to our heart, mind and soul.

## April 11

Let not our hearts be troubled,
for You will not leave us orphans.
You will give us another helper that will abide in us,
the Spirit of truth may dwell within our hearts together.

## April 12

My heart is weak and has no power of its own
and does not wish to become a heart of stone.
It needs Your courage, strength, and love
to carry on, for without You, my heart is lost and gone.

## April 13

May we ask Love to direct our way, thinking and
actions, asking that it be divorced
from self-pity, dishonesty or self-seeking motives
and that it rekindles the love,
to do what is right and good.

## April 14

You are my eternal desire
For You truly inspire and set hearts on fire.
May my soul always be Yours for hire.

## April 15

I ask Love to take away my difficulties:
my suspicious nature
my pride, fear, and insecurities
my anger, self-pity, self-seeking,
and my self-righteous behavior
and any other character flaws of mine that go unchecked or unnoticed and that get in the way of my usefulness to others.

## April 16

Help me not to be chained to my circumstances
and gain Your perspective,
enabling me to distinguish between
what is important
and what is not,
receiving awareness of your presence in my life and the lives of others.

## April 17

Taking minibreaks from this world
to be still in Your presence and hear your voice,
we find hidden treasures in listening
and rich blessings through actively seeking
Your loving guidance.

## April 18

Love asks us to lighten up and laugh within its presence
for it has something far better planned for us
than our own plan.

## April 19

Anxiety will wrap me up in my own thoughts
robbing me of any joy and kindness I may find
in the moment.
Seek the presence of Love with a whisper
and I am free.

## April 20

A grateful and merry heart is good medicine for the soul.

# April 21

If I struggle with a concept of the power of Love,
may I look up into the night sky on a starlit night
and its incredible design and ponder
the wonderful creation of it all.

# April 22

Your loving spirit within us is our tutor,
gently guiding and helping us through our day.
Thank you.

## April 23

Thank You, for You make it possible for me to become my true self and hopefully help someone else become theirs. For You have made Your presence present.

## April 24

Love's soothing words of peace is
not the voice of accusation.
You speak to us in the tones of love that transform
our minds with a gentle uplifting spirit that
convicts cleanly with truth.

## April 25

Love seeks to shine in our lives
and the people around us.
May we open up the door to the light of Love.

## April 26

When prayer becomes a daily practice
I find myself more serene
and have a purpose
and place in this world.

## *April 27*

---

Where the spirit of Love is, there is liberty.

## *April 28*

---

Let me hear and feel
Your loving spirit washing and watching over me, guiding and guarding my thoughts and actions throughout this day.

## April 29

When we refuse to grumble in the midst of our
struggles, we are a twinkle in the eye of Love
and Love looks upon us with a sweet smile.

## April 30

May we draw water from the wells of
salvation and grace
and have hope, joy, and peace in our hearts.

# Reflections

# May

# May

### Breathe

Breathe in the air,
Start to care,
Look at the waves and sea,
Mountains, forest and trees,
See the events all around,
For nature is abound,
Revealing her secrets.
Joy, happiness,
Wisdom and power
Are everywhere to be found,
As we open our eyes, we see
What life and nature are offering
IS TRULY SOUND

## May 1

When we decide on a course of action
that is, in line with love, nothing can stop it.
we may encounter many obstacles
but not to be discouraged-
never give up.
with Love's help we will overcome,
our journey may not be easy,
but if we are on the right path
Love is ever present
and is in the timing of events.
may we only ask for guidance on this path forward,
moment by moment and let love set the pace.

## May 2

Whenever I am afraid, I will trust in You
for You have made your presence present.

## May 3

May we use the talents given us and find value
in sharing, and not to own or possess,
but to treasure that we are able to work
and to help others.

## May 4

You are our sunshine.
May we come to know how much You love us.

# May 5

Let me hear Your loving kindness in the morning
and may I trust in You
showing me the way I should walk throughout the day.

# May 6

Through gratitude and trust
You give us a new loving pattern that
revolutionizes our lives.

# May 7

As the fragrance of your knowledge diffuses over many,
may it lead to an aroma of life for all.

# May 8

In Your light we see how precious is
Your loving kindness
for children of men can put their trust
in the shadow of Your wings and be satisfied
and find fullness and become whole.
What a gift!

## May 9

Do I think I can tell Heaven from Hell,
have I traded hot ashes for trees,
peace of mind for a disease,
comfort for change,
a walk in the park for a mind in the dark.
May I exchange my dark past for a new light,
that over time, makes me alright.

## May 10

Love invites us to know its ways and learn its virtues.
As we connect to its loving presence
we grow in true wholeness.

## May 11

No one can know the depths
of my troubled soul
like You
and how to lead me to a path of healing
like You

## May 12

You give awareness of life that I've never felt before.

## May 13

May I take responsibility for my anger
and not blame or shame another.

## May 14

Love says I will hold your right hand,
fear not, be at peace, for I will help you.

## May 15

I used to run from you, now I run to you.
For you see me from afar and you are my guiding star.

## May 16

A thankful heart and grateful attitude
is a safeguard that allows me to see
your presence shining in all my circumstances.
Thank you for this gift.

## May 17

When gratitude and love are intertwined,
we are blessed with the finest emotion we can have,
ongoing love.

## May 18

Love, help us to have the courage to express gratitude
and love in all our affairs.

## May 19

I have always based how I valued myself on what I had accomplished.
By taking time to appreciate others enriches my day, regardless of my achievements.

## May 20

May we trust in You
and the path You have laid out before us
that we may be aware of the Blessings in Your Presence that lay ahead on this path of life,
for You show us fullness and peace, no matter what our circumstances are.

## May 21

Thank you for being my companion, friend and teacher and an opportunity for a loving lesson to be learned every day of life.

## May 22

May we commit ourselves to this loving presence, and wait patiently to receive the true desires of our heart

# May 23

Love - You give principles to live by, spiritual in nature,
as we seek this stairway into the heavens
You lead us on the paths we should go.

# May 24

As sound, light, and nature give us new
and wonderful insight,
we find answers to our plight.

## May 25

Your loving spirit does its best work in us,
transforming and renewing our mind, body and spirit.
When we spend time with You,
You help us understand one moment at a time.
Let us not miss this beautiful enrichment of our lives.

## May 26

Love is a giver of life
it pours out its life for us and
giving is in love's nature.
May we spend more time in Love's presence
learning when and how to give.

## May 27

When I look into myself
I find that I have placed my self-worth
on my accomplishments and what others
thought of me.
I was always working to become
the center of attention or hiding in the back of the
room. Taking time to appreciate
another human being enriches my day.
May I look for opportunities to share appreciation
and love with the people around me.
To focus on Your loving presence
that in You, we will find peace.
May we open up the book of Love
for You have told us these things.

## May 28

Let us open up the Book of Love to focus
on Your Loving Presence
for You have told us these things that in You
we will find peace.

## May 29

My failures can be a source for blessings,
humbling me and giving me empathy for others
in their weakness
best of all, my weakness, highlights
my dependence on You.
May I trust and believe in you
and watch to see what You will do.

## May 30

Love sees us as a glass onion,
peeling back the layers till things become clear.

# May 31

The most harmful secrets
are those in which we keep to
and from ourselves.

# June

# June

### The Human Race

May we have the insight to stop being the parasite
And sucking the life out of this planet
And live in harmony with it,
For they can see from space
What we are doing to this place,
Knowing that we can't go on at our current pace,
Can't we change? We are the human race.

## June 1

We are wonderfully made, perfectly imperfect.

## June 2

May we dig deep into Love's ways.
May we seek You throughout our days.
May we search for You with all our hearts,
as we would hidden treasure.
For your virtues are how we should measure.

## June 3

In Your eyes we become complete,
in Your eyes we find the one we seek
and we hear Your voice when You speak.

## June 4

Faith comes from right living and good choices.
It's never too late to start living right
and making better choices.
Thank you for your grace.

## June 5

Love is fully acquainted with
sorrows, grief and has suffered.
Love is here to share our pain,
pour out our heart and give us refuge.
May we trust in its safety.

## June 6

Love longs to participate in our lives in mysterious ways,
through understanding and trust and sometimes pain.
Love's training and blessing prepares us
to be a channel of its presence for us and others.

# June 7

May we live and walk with Your loving spirit by our side,
showing kindness, gentleness, and self-control
for these are the virtues of peacefulness,
that I hope I will choose to always show.

# June 8

Love, help us to be of one mind and one accord,
to work together in harmonious action,
to retrieve the one who is lost.

## June 9

Help me to have the self-awareness
to see what my emotional deformities are.
to see how I can cause my own unhappiness
and how I can redirect my thoughts
to loving, healthy ones
through an honest encounter with reality.

## June 10

Am I tongue-tied and twisted,
letting loving words just go whistling by?
May I speak truth and encouragement to those I
meet.

## June 11

Love - You are the gardener of our heart
removing the weeds of pride, worry,
selfishness and doubt.
Through various trials
You train us in the ways of peace
for this affliction is temporary and Your peace
is with us always for the improvement of our character.

## June 12

In Your loving presence we become complete
and have all that we need,
desiring Your loving spirit above all else
we find the best way to live.

# June 13

You meet us in the stillness,
like a searchlight moving to and fro,
You search diligently for those who seek You,
for they are exceedingly precious to You.
And when we meet heart to heart
the result is joyful fulfillment and restoration of our souls.

# June 14

I pray that any words that I speak will lead to You.

# June 15

May we use our gifts for the good of the world.

# June 16

May I learn to live and love again,
to view nature and the world
with a childlike sense of wonder and awe.
To smile, love, and laugh, to experience
the beauty in the moment of it all.

# June 17

You introduce me to myself, not always a pretty sight, but You are gentle and loving in Your ways. Thank you.

# June 18

Do I take precautions
to live my life in a protective bubble
to avoid adverse circumstance that force me
to learn new ways or do I embrace adversity
with trust, faith, openness and lightheartedness?

# June 19

A house that fights within itself will not stand.
Understanding and wisdom will bring peace.

# June 20

Adversity can be my pathway to true peace
when I see it from a new perspective.

# June 21

Am I trusting enough
to let things happen
without striving to predict
or control them?

# June 22

Things I don't like:
for things to change
and
for things to stay the same -
What a dilemma.

# June 23

When I am feeling less than whole
and life feels difficult and draining
You know the depths of my needs
when I open the Book of Love
You are there to let me in
and your presence comforts me

# June 24

May beautiful memories
fill our head on those days
we dread

# June 25

I want to be in that place
where I see Your face in everyone I see,
for You are the Father of light
who makes us right.

# June 26

Our creator has
entered into our
hearts, minds, and lives
in a way which
is indeed
miraculous,
what a miracle.

## June 27

Change the way we
care about
ourselves, see the
needs of others, as
well as our own.

## June 28

You have designed
us to co-create with You,
we do not
hurry this process,
we take it slow in
your loving time
frame and
guidance.

# June 29

The closer we grow to You,
the more we become our true selves,
that You
designed us to be,
thank You for this love,
that guides us
in the ways of love.

May we allow love
and thankfulness to
flow freely from
our hearts.

Love - may You
create in us a clean
heart and renew
a right Spirit within us.

# June 30

Impossible is not impossible, it's a choice.
May I choose wisely.

# Reflections

# July

# July

### Where Fire and Water Meet

At the rising and setting sun,
The waves are up,
So it is to Boomer we run,
To catch those A-frame waves,
That give us exhilaration and fun,
We ride all day until the day is done,
And as we start,
We watch the morning glass glistening
From the morning sun,
It passes over our head,
And we get an amazing feeling that we are one,
And as we shred across the face,
We find solace in this place,
For whether in the barrel or inside the tube,
This is where we go to get aqua lubed,
And as we watch in slow motion,
Our rides form lasting memories of the ocean,
That are with us still,
For we have found a form of meditation in a thrill.

**Dedicated to Mark Holmes and all the body surfers at Boomer, current and past, and to all the wave riders around the world.**

## July 1

May I trust
in Your presence to open up the way before me,
one step at a time,
and relax and enjoy the journey.
Thank you.

## July 2

You prepare us for the day that
stretches out before us,
as we spend quality time with You,
in Your presence,
Through communication,
You equip us for the journey ahead,
for You are our loving companion and guide.

## July 3

You liberate us from self,
you recreate us in the likeness of love.

## July 4

The best times I've experienced in life is when I've lived responsively and responsibly and have felt connected and richly alive.

## July 5

Though we may be oceans apart
May the ripples of Your loving words
Bring us together at Heart!

## July 6

You pull us from a pit of despair and set us upon a rock,
You call us out of darkness into a marvelous light and we become kinder, slower to anger and more loving day by day.

## July 7

I use to run from You,
now I run to You, for You are always there.
You catch me when I fall, time after time.
You keep me from losing my mind.
When we open the Book of Love, You let us in.
You take these broken wings
and teach us to fly again.

## July 8

When I am in that place where I don't want the world to see me, You come to me just where I am, broken, because You want me to know just who You are and that You understand.

## July 9

Your thoughts embrace us
In everlasting love,
You know the plans You have for us,
plans to prosper, to give us hope and a future.
Our Journey Begins
with You
transforming and renewing our minds.
May we give ourselves fully to
this adventure of
Grace.

## July 10

Love - You keep an eye on my heart
before I start my day.
May I always remember to thank you and pray.

# July 11

Love asks, enjoy My presence.
Choose to trust Me in all your circumstance.

# July 12

Self-pity is a false comfort momentarily
screening me from reality,
then like a drug, dragging deeper into a pit of despair,
demanding that I take a bigger dose.
The antidote for this exaggerated suffering is
to help someone less fortunate than me,
even if it's by phone.

# July 13

When I was a child, I had a fleeting glimpse out of the corner of my eye what it meant to become a man, to put away childish things.
Love brings me face to face with what I see dimly now and to be greatly reminded of the birds, flowers, trees, great rivers, and seas.

# July 14

Resentments destroy more people than anything else. I cannot afford to relive old hurts, for they will eventually sicken me -mind, body, and soul- and keep me in the dark.

## July 15

I was a slave to negative behavior patterns.
A loving spirit guided me to a process of letting go.
Today I am given a choice to be free of this bondage of self and open the door to a new freedom.

## July 16

You don't care where we are from, who we are or what we did, only that we learn to Love as You have loved us.

## July 17

Love has a keen observation,
nothing in our lives escapes its sight
It's light shines into our souls and desires
to show us the way we should go

## July 18

Steadiness is Your desire for us,
not to let events throw us off course.
Rather to respond calmly and confidently and to be
at peace within,
for you are with us.

## July 19

May my true ambition be
to live a useful and humble life
under the grace of God.

## July 20

With Your loving kindness, You have drawn us, with an everlasting love you rebuild us and we stand in the Son's light.

Am I prideful when I should be humble? Am I arrogant when I should be kind? Are my words meaningful? Do I criticize and complain when I should be grateful? Are my actions filled with vanity and self-seeking motives or are they understanding, kind, and true?

These are the questions I should ask myself throughout my day.

## July 21

Loves wonderful works satisfies the longing and hurried soul with goodness.
Love transforms children into men and women.

## July 22

The ways of Your love lift us up and put us on high ground, teaching us how to care about others.

## July 23

In the light of your presence, we are able to see the hidden things in our nature.

## July 24

Your loving spirit has pulled me out of despairing pits on several occasions and has sheltered me from the storm. Because of Your compassion, I am not consumed.

# July 25

When doing good deeds, do I seek approval and glory or am I happy just to be of service?
These are the questions I must ask myself.

# July 26

Fear prevents me from experiencing the wonders of life.
Cultivating faith helps my appreciation for beauty, tolerance, forgiveness, service and to be at peace with myself and those around me.

## July 27

Love asks, rest in my stillness while my presence prepares you for this day.
Let the radiant beauty of my glory shine upon you.
Be still in confidence knowing that you are loved.

## July 28

Love - may You pour
yourself into our
emptiness, and
neediness and
fill us with Love's DNA
for You are our
greatest need.

## July 29

Since we are surrounded by so great
a cloud of witnesses,
let us set aside every weight, belief, and difference
which so easily ensnares us and let us run
with endurance in this loving race
working together to be the author and finisher
of peace on this earth.

## July 30

There's a belief:
To acquire it, I only have to stop fighting
and practice as enthusiastically as I can;
-a loving program of right living-

# July 31

Love sweeps us out of the night and into the light.

# August

# August

### Paradise

Though paradise and I rarely meet,
I must be grateful to still be on my feet,
The food I have to eat,
And the people I am fortunate to meet,
So, I will be prepared when paradise and I
do finally meet.

## August 1

It's not the destination that build and test our character, but our journey on the way there.

## August 2

You instruct us and teach us in the way we should go, thank you for your loving guidance.

## August 3

You help me see that any failures I experience in life as a source of empathy for others and You give greater than anything that was lost.

## August 4

Love - You are my guide and my truth.
You teach me important lessons on the path
You have prepared before me.

# August 5

May the windows of heaven open up and let us in and
may we begin to see what we truly can be

# August 6

A humble spirit will retain honor.

## August 7

To be upright is to seek well-being.

## August 8

Help me to have a childlike trust as
You open the way before me,
step by step.
If we lose everything and
gain peace,
we are truly rich, and
we are treasured.

## August 9

Whoever loves wisdom and understanding
make his parents rejoice.

## August 10

The thoughtful and understanding consider the causes of the poor.
The wise hold back their tongue around those who gossip and judge.

## August 11

Help me to love people
As You love them
for my love is limited and full of flaws and manipulation
and Your love truly cares

## August 12

Heaven is not for those who want in, but for those who make the sacrifice to help others get in.

# August 13

Love says, I will give you another helper that will abide with you, the spirit of truth will dwell within you and come to you.

# August 14

Thank You for every cell, every molecule,
for every living creature and creation.
May we celebrate the gift of life.

## August 15

You are the author
and designer of miracles in the making
You breakthrough the barriers we have built
over the years
may we begin to let others in

## August 16

Commit our works to love and our thoughts
will be established.

## August 17

May our scars become stars
May our messes become messages
May our failures lead to success
May our adversity lead
to good character and compassion
May our life experiences lead us
To truth, understanding, and becoming
Kinder and more loving human beings.

## August 18

When intelligence speaks,
Wisdom listens.

## August 19

How we handle our failures and setbacks
is our true measure of success.

## August 20

Impossible is not a fact or a declaration,
it's an opinion, daring us to expand our potential.

## August 21

Self-searching and self-improvement builds a ladder of honesty and hope to find the courage to live with a spirit of readiness to serve others.

## August 22

May I ask You for the courage
To speak the truth in a
Loving, gentle way
When Your hand leads me to do so

## August 23

May we come to know You are out there and that You hear our prayers.

## August 24

I need help because I don't know how to be understanding, when I don't feel understood.
I don't know how to be comforting, when I don't feel comforted.
I don't know how to be loving, when I don't feel loved.
Help my heart, mind, and soul become whole.

## August 25

May Your loving spirit
Touch Our hearts and protect us
From ourselves.

## August 26

Learning to observe
all things and
Comprehend them,
with loving wisdom
and responsibility,
is a gift to be
treasured.

## August 27

Let our understanding be a path to truth.

## August 28

True freedom comes from living with love as our guide and doing what is right.

## August 29

As I seek your words and guidance my attitude and actions change and You reveal the things I need to change and grow towards.

## August 30

The words of love are living and powerful. They are a discerner of thoughts and intents of the heart. Love opens the eyes to see who we are and what we can become with its guidance.

# August 31

In your presence we become a reservoir for Your spirit to flow and as it streams through us,
it permeates us with love, joy and peace and creates a bubbling spring that spills onto others.

# September

# September

**More**

We have so much more than what they had a hundred years before,
Why are our attitudes so poor,
And why is the gap so large between the rich and the poor,
And why can't we seem to get along anymore;
Please help us understand why it is we always want more
And how Your love fills our desire for what we truly long for

## September 1

You are stimulating the synapses and cells of my brain, revitalizing my perceptions, creating portals of new awareness and love that are invigorating and alive.

## September 2

For you are healed and have returned to the shepherd and over-seer of your soul.

## September 3

Anxious and fearful thoughts melt away in the light of Your presence and we find the deepest fulfillment of our heart in You alone.

## September 4

Though I miss the mark and fall short, You are there to pick me up and put me back on Your loving path.

## September 5

You prepare the day before us. You eagerly await our waking up and rejoice when we glance and consciously desire Your loving ways.

## September 6

As the one who loved You, You have also loved us. May we abide in Your love.

## September 7

We neither look forward or behind,
we instead focus our attention on You and You fully
equip us for whatever journey awaits us.

## September 8

You are the loving light that guides us.
Thank You.

# September 9

May Your loving light grow in the dark areas of our lives and awaken our souls.

# September 10

May I learn to help some and harm none.

## September 11

May our dark become someone's light and by so doing we are freed and our lives become meaningful.

## September 12

In the light of Your perspective, we discover treasures in our trials.

## September 13

What I see in others I manifest in myself.

## September 14

You put Your thoughts into our mind and a song in our heart.
In Your presence we are blessed with irrepressible joy.
Thank you.

## September 15

Love takes pleasure in those who hope in loves mercy and we walk in a new and wonderful light.

## September 16

Love's illuminating light is nearer and far more real than the world we see and desires to show us the invisible things we should richly value.

## September 17

Thank You for freeing me from the cell of my own mind made hell and making me well.

## September 18

May we come boldly into the light, choosing to enjoy Your loving presence within.

## September 19

May the light of Your presence shine upon us and be visible to those around us.

## September 20

May we become a reflection of Your loving presence that we may live and love together.

# September 21

Because of Love's great mercy,
love desires to shine its light into the dark condition
of mankind and bring it into the light.

# September 22

The world is vibrantly alive with Love's presence through sights, sounds, thoughts impressions and scriptures.
There is no limit to the variety of ways Love can communicate with us. Its light can shine into the dark and deepest sorrows and weave it into a pattern for good.

## September 23

You instruct and teach us in the way we should go. You guide us with your insight.

## September 24

Let me seek and hear Your loving kindness in the morning for You lift up my soul and show me in the way I should go.

## September 25

In our constant thought of others, Love meets our needs.

## September 26

May we make a home for the light of Love to live and love through us.

## September 27

May we work in rhythm with Your loving guidance for it is a privilege and a joyous lifeline.

## September 28

When I obsess on my past, I give it the power to rule my present. Help me see the goodness in the moment.

## September 29

May we relax in Your healing presence and let Your light shine softly in to our lives, allowing us to see more clearly.

## September 30

Love does not wish to retaliate and cares more for the feelings of others than for its own.

# Reflections

# October

# *October*

**Wisdom**

May the beauty of the rising and setting suns
Always light our path
May the starlit nights always shine in our eyes
And may God's love and wisdom always be
Our prize

# October 1

Love delights in our enjoyment
of things true, noble, right, pure, loving, and
admirable. As we think and do these things
the light of love shines brighter day by day.

# October 2

May you teach us to practice love as You love, understanding as You understand and forgiving as You forgive.

# October 3

You heal broken bodies, broken minds, broken hearts, broken lives and broken relationships.
There is immense healing power in the light of Your very presence as we live close to You.
Thank you.

# October 4

When I reach a point in life that I don't need a magnificent life to see the magnificence in life, I then have a chance of finding peace.

# October 5

When my mind is unfocused, it is vulnerable to a downward pull.
May my focus be on the light of Your presence,
my constant companion that brings sparkle into my routine days.

# October 6

May I put away my scars and set my sight on the stars.

## October 7

May I stay connected to Your loving presence throughout my day,
through prayer and quiet communication
for You give me strength and guidance.

## October 8

I've been a victim of a selfish kind of love, thinking only of my own welfare and it now scares me to think and feel this way.

## October 9

May I desire to grow in the light of a selfless kind of love.

## October 10

May the light of Your spirit shine deeply into our souls and guide us in the way we should go.

# October 11

Help me to live and work in collaboration with the light of Your presence.

# October 12

May we desire to be a conduit for Your loving spirit, enjoying this intimate adventure You offer, living through us.

## October 13

For some of our poets have said, for in Him we live and move and have our being.

## October 14

If we are chained, let these links connect us to hope, trusting, waiting, knowing and seeing of loves return to our hearts, minds and souls.

# October 15

Your path is like the shining sun, shining brighter unto a perfect day.

# October 16

The cliffs are shear and very high, with Your help, we are sure to get by.
Thank you.

## October 17

May You live in our hearts and may Your loving thoughts occupy our minds that we may learn to become kind, dignified and true.

## October 18

Christ, please forgive us for all the misery and pain we inflict upon ourselves and one another.
Please help us change for there is no future in this.

# October 19

As we go along this path of life may we realize our deepest desire is finding satisfaction in Your loving presence.
Thank you, Jesus.

# October 20

May we bask in the Son's light, for He is a true companion.

# October 21

Give our mind a break from its habitual judging, from judgements about this situation or that situation, this person or that person, ourselves as if judging is our main function in life. For I have squandered many hours away, wanting things my way.

# October 22

In the twinkling of an eye, You pass by and for a moment we get that amazing feeling that we are one.

## October 23

May loves face shine upon us and be gracious.

## October 24

Your presence is all around, our prayers have been recorded and honored.
Your blessings are coming.

# October 25

Love asks – don't forget me when we fall apart, just call my name and I'll put us back together at heart. Thank You, Jesus.

# October 26

Mercy and truth preserve and loving kindness upholds.

# October 27

Love - thank You for showing us compassion and understanding and allowing us to see a new and different way.

# October 28

You are the creator of the entire universe, yet Your loving desire is to make Your humble home in our hearts. You work on our inner selves as we do our part in the outer world.

# October 29

The light of Jesus's love calls. If we hide from You how can our love grow?

# October 30

As we build these stairways to the heavens, may our hearts be filled with the light of Your understanding and love.

# October 31

Even great sinners can be transformed when we turn our passions towards a loving creator and forgiveness and may we seek the knowledge and awareness of his loving presence.

# November

# November

### Scars

May our scars become someone's stars, may our dark become someone's light, and may our messes become a message, and may this change break the chains.

## November 1

Your peace
surpasses all
understanding and
seeks to guard our
hearts and minds,

May we trust and
be grateful for this.

## November 2

I do my best thinking through the help of others.

# November 3

You are the light that shines through the trees and that removes me from my disease.

# November 4

I ask that my thinking be cleared of self-pity and self-seeking motives. That my mental faculties be placed on a loving path and a higher plane of assurance that is cleared of wrong motives.

# November 5

It is our soul that You love rather than our appearance or performance.
When we center our lives around You, we feel Your presence.

# November 6

You give your loving spirit to us freely that we may learn to love in a new and wonderful whole way.

# November 7

No matter what losses we have experienced Your presence and companionship can comfort us and as You comfort us we become a channel on which You comfort others and we are blessed.

# November 8

Am I learning not to measure my giving to my getting, accepting that the act of giving is its own reward and learn to care deeply for the welfare of others.

# November 9

When the clouds of my mind start to clear, my ears are then able to hear and when I am lost at sea, may I feel Your presence here with me.

# November 10

Do I become so heavenly that I am no earthly good and so earth bound that I am no heavenly good. Help me to find this balance.

# November 11

Your loving relationship with us is saturated with grace, Your glorious grace and our salvation are inseparable when we come to you with a willingness to change.

# November 12

You have made known the ways of life; You will make us full of joy in Your presence.

# November 13

In the twinkling of an eye, You soften our fears and give us a glimpse of life without fears and for that moment we stand in the Son's light and life has new meaning.

# November 14

Our world is rigged with massive distractions and when we have wandered away, Your loving presence is patiently waiting for us to initiate communication with You and we can rejoice in these tiny triumphs that increasingly light up our day.

# November 15

We have this treasure in clay jars to show that this power is from God and not from us. We are hard pressed, but not crushed, perplexed but not in despair, persecuted but not abandoned. Struck down but not destroyed.

Thus, our weakness and woundedness become treasures to others, to us and to God's kingdom for light to shine out of darkness.

# November 16

May we cast all our cares upon You, for You care and help us to have a thankful and grateful attitude that we may see Your blessings.

# November 17

A grateful and thankful heart protects us from despair, discouragement and self-pity and helps our love to grow stronger and brighter.

# November 18

You laid down your life for our shame, Jesus, for which the whole family in heaven is named.

# November 19

May Your presence grow stronger and soak into our inner being that we may trust You with all our heart, mind and soul.

# November 20

Paul wrote 'Whatever is true, whatever is noble, whatever is right…'.
Think about these things…

# November 21

May I learn how to change resentments into acceptance, fear into hope, anger into love, without undue expectations.

# November 22

May we inspire understanding, compassion and love within ourselves and others.

## November 23

I have allowed past failures and successes to define who I am. May I allow God's love and truth to change me into who I can be.

## November 24

Tender mercy has visited us to give light to those who sit in darkness and the shadow of death, to guide our feet into the way of peace.

# November 25

"Let thankfulness and Trust
be our guide through this day."

# November 26

When I familiarize myself
and practice spiritual principles in my life
and offer a helping hand to
someone in need,
I find I get recharged
with indescribable
gratitude and peace

Through continual communication
with You
we find an adequate supply of
miracles
to help us rise about our circumstances,
and with a thankful heart
we find peace.

# November 27

Thank You Jesus for gradually and continually filling us with Your loving presence of peace, for the less of us we are, the more of You we become.

# November 28

We have this treasure that the power of good may work through us.

# November 29

You are our helper that teaches us all things. You give to us not as the world gives, so let our hearts
be at peace.

# November 30

In one form or another, my character defects can appear daily –
self-condemnation, anger, fear, hurt feelings,
giving up or grandiosity.
May I be grateful to God for the days I'm able to recognize and change these character defects.

# Reflections

# December

# *December*

**Love**

Love may You take this broken mind and broken heart,
And give it a fresh new start,
For it has lost its place,
And its ability to embrace
And it longs again to meet Love face-to-face.

# December 1

You have created and gifted us with a creative soul.
May we listen intimately to the world around us
And allow our gifts to richly flourish and unfold.

# December 2

Loving gifts
sometimes come
wrapped in trials,
help us to rejoice in
adversity
and
find peace.

# December 3

The sense of sight is a spectacular gift You have given us. Let us not minimize it by judging and complaining of what we see, but to see the beauty that abounds when our sight is in line with Yours and we are blessed with a joyful and grateful heart.

# December 4

May we turn our frowns upside down and make ourselves someone others want to be around.

# December 5

May we read scripture, for it is the star of guidance illuminating our hearts and enlightening our minds.

# December 6

Jesus, may Your loving spirit enter into us in a way which is indeed miraculous and change us from the inside out that we may see and live in a new and wonderfully different way.

# December 7

Happiness isn't something I can demand. It comes upon me quietly while helping others.

# December 8

Nothing comes to pass,
sitting on one's ass
so may we ask where to start
and open our heart to doing our part.

# December 9

How can we dance or sleep while our heads and hearts are turning and burning?
Let us show we care and give to Him what belongs to Him, let's give it back.

# December 10

Take me as I am, change me until all of me is gone and only you remain.
For the less of me and the more of You the better off I am.

# December 11

May I allow you access to my mind, heart and soul that you may overtake me and make me completely whole, that I may begin to understand the depths, width, heights and length of Your love.

# December 12

With joy let us draw water from the wells of salvation and grace.

# December 13

Under Your wing you show us how to care and we are safe and secure in God's hands when we open up the Book of Love and read this book.

# December 14

May we be a pathway for You to love others through us.

## December 15

God is love and He who abides in Love,
Love abides in Him.

## December 16

May the radiance of Your love fall gently upon us and soak into the innermost parts of our being until we are one.

## December 17

Thank You for making us imperfect so that we may show compassion. Save us from being judgmental.

## December 18

Do not be concerned with our physical stature or appearance, for man sees with his eyes, love looks at the heart.

# December 19

Your loving words are a lamp to our feet and a light to our path.

# December 20

Love is the light that came into the world that anyone who believes in Him should not stay in darkness.

# December 21

Hope does not disappoint because love has been poured out into our hearts and minds and given through a spirit of patience and perseverance.

# December 22

Love and obedience died a criminal's death so we could be adorned and blessed with its perfection, its DNA, that its ways may be written on our hearts and minds.

# December 23

Thank You for loving us when no one else would, help us to return the favor.

# December 24

Your loving training of befriending our problems opens our minds to the benefits flowing from difficulties. Your wisdom is sufficient to bring good out of them.

# December 25

May we receive Your peace
abundantly and thankfully,
for it is a rare treasure,
dazzling in radiant and delicate beauty,
what a gift.
Don't wait for things to be perfect
before I decide to enjoy it

# December 26

When I have experienced enough emotional pain,
through my own failed attempts to fix things myself,
I become wiling to surrender my life to your loving
presence and learn how to truly live.

# December 27

Help us not to go it alone and know that You and I together can handle the circumstances we face.

# December 28

Through the light of your presence and the experience of your spirit we are able to face any problems with good cheer.

# December 29

We were created for
good works, that
we should walk in them.
We are Love's workmanship,
Prepared beforehand

Thank you.

# December 30

You enable us to distinguish what is important.
Thank You.

# December 31

This New Year's brings us the opportunity for a new day every day of the year.

# Afterword

## Insecurity

Insecurity and fear can lead us to self-centeredness
And on to alcohol and drug abuse
Which can eventually heighten our insecurity, fears, and self-seeking motives
Isolating us from friends, family, and society at large.
A high price for a low life.
Paying top dollar to live in squalor.
This behavior can go on for many a season,
And as we build this wall of a mind-made prison,
Our vision becomes blurred,
Our reality obscurred,
And Our actions absurd,
The insanity settles in and makes its home
And we find ourselves totally alone
And there seems to be no way out
Inside our heads, we shout:
*I can't go on*
This becomes our only familiar song
What is wrong? - What is wrong? - I can't go on

Knowing that the way we are living is wrong
To change meant we would have to change
And do something new
We can no longer sit in this sea of resentment and self-pity,

This soul-sickening disease
Doing what we please
And flows on to others like stormy seas,
If we wanted something we never had
We would have to do something we've never done
A willingness to believe.

We found we could be relieved
Of this soul-sickening pain
That we might once again become sane
And stop causing others and ourselves
Unecessary anguish and pain,
Sometimes, it's through great pain,
that we are able to make great gain
But not without the strain,
Can we expect to obtain and sub-stain,
From the terrible and demoralizing afflication
Of addiction
May we come to believe in the power of Love

Lightning Source UK Ltd.
Milton Keynes UK
UKHW040847021222
413231UK00001B/5